UNFRIENDLY NATIVES OF THE PACIFIC

AND OTHER FASCINATING TALES OF CREATURES OF THE DEEP

ARO PUBLISHING

Written by Glen Wright
Edited by Carol Murphy
Consultant Vera Nielsen
 Former Vice-President Utah Library Association
Illustrations by Keith Christensen

First published by ARO Publishing Inc., 1981

Library of Congress Cataloging in Publication Data
Wright, Glen.
   Unfriendly natives of the Pacific and other fascinat-
ing tales of the creatures of the deep

   (Fascinating tales of the Pacific)
   Bibliography: p.
   Contents: Te Rokea! tiger of the sea—Unfriendly
natives of the Pacific—The snorkeler—(etc.)
   1. Dangerous marine animals—South Pacific Ocean—
Juvenile literature. 2. Marine fauna—South Pacific
Ocean—Juvenile literature. 3. Fishing—South Pacific
Ocean—Juvenile literature. (1. Dangerous marine
animals. 2. Marine animals. 3. South Pacific Ocean)
I. Title. II. Series: Wright, Glen. Fascinating tales
of the Pacific.
QL138.W74   591.6   81-12776
ISBN 0-89868-123-5 (pbk.)   AACR2
ISBN 0-89868-116-2 (lib. bdg.)

CONTENTS

Page
4   TE ROKEA! TIGER OF THE SEA
16   UNFRIENDLY NATIVES OF THE PACIFIC
24   THE SNORKELER: A STRANGE FISH
28   FISHING IS A DARING ART
38   THE PEARL DIVERS OF MANIHIKI
42   PALOLO IS RISING!

PHOTO CREDITS

COVER PHOTO:
RUSS KINNE, PHOTO RESEARCHERS.

GLEN WRIGHT:
PAGES 5, 21.

PHOTO RESEARCHERS:
PAGES 7, 8, 15, 17b, 19, 22, 27, 29, 33, 35, 39.

NICK VAZZANA:
PAGES 9, 12, 32.

BISHOP MUSEUM:
PAGE 17a, 18.

MARION J. HEAD:
PAGE 23.

JAMES SIERS:
PAGES 43, 45.

TE ROKEA! TIGER OF THE SEA

The Pacific Ocean is home for nearly every variety of shark known. There are more than 200 kinds. They live all over the sea, but mostly in the South.

South Sea Islanders have great respect for sharks. They know how to deal with them. Many of their favorite stories are about sharks.

Samoan fisherman in a dugout canoe.

Ten Ave's canoe jumped as if it had hit a reef.

Then the boat rose high out of the water.

Instantly Ten knew what was under the boat. Te Rokea! (Tay Row-kay-aw) Shark!

He sat down and grabbed the paddle. He moved the boat to one side. Its keel slid off the back of the 15 foot monster.

The big fish stayed on the surface. It swam slowly in a circle around him, each time coming closer. Ten Ave panicked. The shark was hungry. Did it know that there were fish in the canoe?

Ten, a Tuvalu Islander, had put to sea that morning before dawn. His luck had been good. He had caught many tuna and flying fish. He was preparing to start back to his home in Funafuti when the shark bumped his boat.

He began to feed the shark. He threw the fish as far away as possible. Then he paddled madly toward shore. Te Rokea dashed for each morsel and then returned to the canoe. Even after swallowing the last tuna, it was unsatisfied.

Finally it swam alongside and stared at him. Ten knew then that the big shark was going to attack his boat. In that one fearful glance it had taken a picture of its prey. It knew where to strike.

Sand shark. Photograph by John S. Flannery/P.R.

Ten was afraid, but determined. He was an experienced seaman. He knew a trick that might save him. He filled his big plastic water bottle. The mere act of putting his hands in the sea chilled his nerves.

Then he threw the bottle far out over the waves and dug in his paddle. As the canoe leaped forward he looked back. The shark was chewing vigorously on the bottle. It tossed its head from side to side trying to unstick it from its teeth. Never before had Ten paddled his canoe so furiously. He was going so fast the boat skidded onto the beach when it arrived at Funafuti. How wonderful it was to be ashore, safe from Te Rokea's big jaws!

Sharks are the most vicious killers and the greediest eaters of all sea animals.

Some sharks, such as the whale variety, are as long as 50 feet. The smallest shark is probably the black tip, about five feet long.

Grey Nurse shark. Photograph by Tom McHugh/P.R.

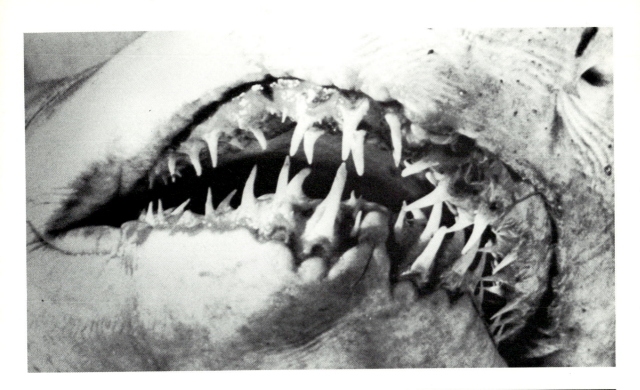

Authorities disagree about the meanness of sharks. Some argue that they are just naturally vicious and bad tempered. But others say they appear so only because they are always hungry. Food goes swiftly through their stomachs. They must eat continually, as they burn up so much energy. They say the hammerhead is tame because it lives in lagoons where food is plentiful.

The shark's mouth is beneath its head. But it does not have to turn onto its back to bite. Just ask anyone who has been nipped by a shark!

There are no teeth like sharks' teeth. Some are long and sharp. Others are broad and flat. They are all dangerous instruments. The jaws in which they are imbedded are powerful, and some are big enough to swallow a human being.

How well sharks can rip and tear is illustrated in Hemingway's story Old Man and the Sea. How vicious they can be is the theme of Benchley's Jaws.

How fast they can swim is anybody's guess. They glide through the depths at great speed, and they can move like this for long distances.

Some sharks lay eggs, but most of them bear their young live.

Natives of the Solomon Islands see sharks in a different light.

Solomon Islands boys and girls sometimes even make friends with sharks. This happens only on certain small islands. There sharks gather to rest in quiet little bays along the shores.

When Solomon Islanders kill pigs, they remove the bladders and fill them with air. When dried, these balloons are tough and bouncy.

The children tie them onto long sticks. They go to where the sharks are basking in the shallow water. Standing on the sand at the water's edge the children tap the fish on their heads and backs with the balloons. The sharks like this. If none of them bite the bladders, the children slip into the water and swim among them. They are never harmed. Sometimes the sharks play games by nosing the balloons around among themselves.

The following is a favorite story in the Solomons.

As a little girl Firiba (Fee-ree-ba) had always played with sharks. When she was 16 she swam to another island where such play was not a custom. She became friends with a girl her age named Aloa.

Together they started to swim to Firiba's island, chatting gaily. They neared shore in the evening.

Suddenly Firiba turned to ask Aloa why she was so silent. Her new friend was not there.

Firiba swam on, weeping sadly. After a while a shark appeared beside her and accompanied her home.

The islanders telling this story don't say what happened to Aloa. But you know, don't you?

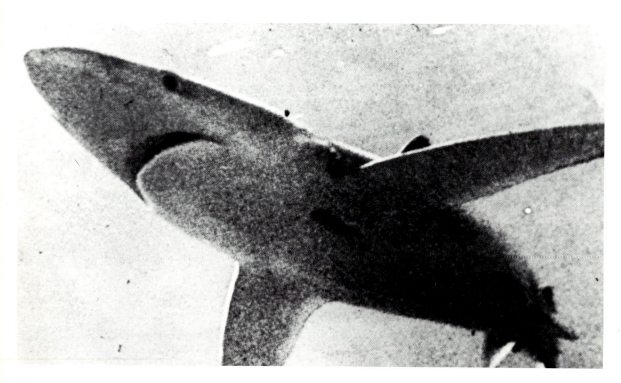

Another place sharks like is the cold sea around Stewart Island, at the southern tip of New Zealand. At certain times of the year they gather there by the thousands to feed and reproduce. The fishermen of Stewart Island hate the sharks.

A Stewart Island fisherman caught a big fish, but never landed it in his boat. A shark took it off the hook. Angry, the man grabbed his rifle and shot at the next shark he saw. It disappeared, wounded.

In a few minutes the man's boat rose in the water and rocked dangerously. The wounded shark was under it. If the fisherman had fallen out, he would never have been seen again.

Another fisherman struck a fish-stealing shark on the nose with an oar. The enraged creature began to bite chunks out of the man's boat. The man barely got it back to shore without sinking.

There are many fish in the waters around Stewart Island. But when the sharks gather there, the fishermen might as well stay home. They won't get many fish. The sharks will.

This is why they are called tigers of the sea.

Blacktip Reef sharks. Photograph by Tom McHugh/P.R.

UNFRIENDLY NATIVES OF THE PACIFIC

Nature in the South Seas is usually beautiful and peaceful. But it can be dangerous and sometimes deadly. Many "unfriendly natives" lurk in this immense ocean. The terrible shark you know about. Here are more that you'd better watch out for.

Coral.

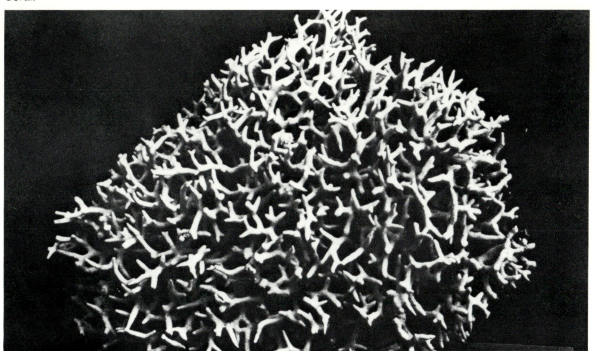

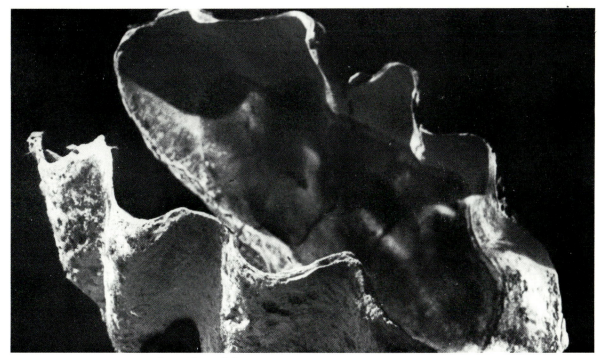

Giant clam. Photograph by Russ Kinne/P.R.

A swimmer brushes against a jellyfish floating like a bubble on the waves. Suddenly he is half paralyzed with pain. The creature has stung him.

A fisherman steps on a cone shell on the beach. It shoots a tiny poisoned arrow into his foot. The hurt is intense.

In both cases death may result.

An unfriendly pink worm inflicts painful stings with its hair. The little six-inch creature is covered with needle-sharp, gold-colored whiskers.

An Australian ship cruised south of Hawaii. Its crew sat down to a meal of fresh-caught fish. Four hours later they were all desperately ill.

Red snapper fish may be poison when caught in one place, and not in another. Or dangerous one day and safe the next. Professor Albert Banner of the University of Hawaii's marine laboratory has a theory. He says the fish become toxic when they eat a certain kind of seaweed.

Cone shells, various types.

Portuguese Man-of-War. (Jellyfish) Photograph by Jack Dermid, National Audubon Society/P.R.

Because of this a fishing industry is impossible in some areas. Around Johnson Island three-fourths of the fish may be poisonous. Near Saipan practically all of them are, in the opinion of Professor T.T. Kennedy, of Ardmore College in New Zealand.

Waders, swimmers and skin-divers must beware of the hatpin urchin. Its spines grow a foot long. They are barbed, jet-black, hollow and filled with poison. Another dangerous reef pest is the crown of thorns starfish.

Curiously, the most venomous animal of all never bites. It is the daddacaluci (da-da-caw-loo-chee), or black and white seasnake. It is deadlier than the cobra. But it is so mild-mannered that it may be safely handled. Fijian children play with it all the time.

Black and white sea snake.

Fijian with Crown of Thorns starfish.

The octopus is usually tame. Nevertheless it sometimes becomes fierce and harmful. Rob Wright, Fijian fishing and skin-diving writer, tells of the time a large, male octopus attacked a woman who had caught its mate. She almost died from his vicious bites.

Coral is just as perilous as it is beautiful. A tiny scratch can cause serious infection and nauseating illness. Gangrene sets in swiftly if coral cuts are deep.

It is risky to get too close to an open giant sea clam. Some of these are as large as five feet across. They may weigh as much as a half ton. All are stuck fast to the seabed and are hard to move.

Swimmers could be caught in the vise-like jaws and drowned. It is said that pearl divers carry knives on slings around their necks. If a clam seizes a leg or arm, the diver may have to cut it off to escape.

Octopus. Photograph by Russ Kinne/P.R.

Coral Marine Life.

THE SNORKELER: A STRANGE FISH

South Sea islanders were the world's first under-water spear fishermen. As soon as they had glass, they made diving goggles with frames carved from wood or shell.

When spearguns, underwater cameras, rubber fins, snorkels and aqualungs came along, the islanders used them.

South Pacific island reefs, tidal lagoons and warm seas are ideal for underwater sport. Where there are reefs there are fish. These colorful coral formations make exciting pictures for submarine photographers.

Warm water fish are wary and have to be carefully stalked. They change colors to blend with their environment, making them hard to see.

Wherever there are fish there are sharks. They search every grotto and crevasse for food. They love to attend a fish-spearing. Sharks are seldom interested in the snorkeling or aqualunging fisherman, but they take great interest in the fish on the spear.

However, they are unpredictable. They may choose instead the big, strange fish with the bug eyes and webbed tail fins — the fisherman!

The spear zipped through the water and pierced the big sea bass in the stomach.

It was a bad shot. The aqualunger had aimed for just behind the gills. But the fish had moved at the last moment.

The underwater fisherman released his spear-gun to float to the surface. Then he went for his catch.

But he didn't move fast enough.

A shark beat him to it.

It curved upward from a cave where it had been lurking. The huge, gray predator made off with the bass and spear. The fisherman had slipped the spear's line off his wrist just in the nick of time. Otherwise he would have been taken with the bass.

And so it goes with the underwater fisherman, cameraman or observer. Never a dull moment down there in the deep. There is always the possibility of an unusual adventure. Danger, too!

Pacific islanders have always been at home in the sea. They have harvested the ocean as farmers harvest the land.

Traditionally they have rowed out in canoes to where reefs meet the open sea. With 12 foot spears in hand they have scanned the bottom for fish. When they spotted fish, they dived and impaled them on their lances. Some, such as the grouper, have weighed as much as 300 pounds.

One of the most famous of underwater explorers was the late Rob Wright of Fiji. He tells some interesting stories in his book Hook, Line and Sinker.

One day Wright came upon a school of mullet down by a reef. The big fish were surrounded by a swarm of little ones, called wrasse. The tiny fish were nuzzling gills and nipping here and there at the mullets' bodies.

Many big fish, such as the mullet, are infested with parasites. The wrasse clean off the parasites.

The wrasse perform this service for several varieties of larger fish. These are all carniverous, but they never eat wrasse. There's appreciation for you!

Queensland Grouper. Photograph by Tom McHugh/P.R.

FISHING IS A DARING ART

Fishing in the Pacific Ocean is dangerous work. But it is necessary as the islanders need the meat.

Therefore, they go fishing whether they like it or not. To make it safer and more fun they use some clever methods, as illustrated by the following story.

Octopus. Photograph by Russ Kinne/P.R.

A huge octopus lurked in a cave deep in the sea by the Kiribati (Kee-ree-baw-tee) Islands. Its eyes gleamed in the blue water.

Two young boys stood on the cliff above. They were hungry for octopus meat cooked in coconut cream. So was their family. Delicious!

"Go get one," their father told them.

The boys waited until the morning breeze stopped and the sea was calm. By that time the sun was up high and shone deep into the water. Its light revealed the octopus hiding in a coral cave. Its long tentacles waved in big circles.

One of the boys dived. He swam directly toward the devil-fish. When he got close, it seized him with long, powerful arms.

When that happened, his brother dived down. He grabbed the octopus' head and bit deeply into the soft top. His teeth penetrated its brain.

The dead octopus let go of the coral rocks to which it had been clinging. Its captor swam swiftly ashore with it still wrapped around his body.

According to Arthur Grimble, in the book Pattern of Islands, the Kiribatians always used to catch octopus that way. But not anymore. The present generation considers it too dangerous.

James Siers, New Zealand writer and photographer, wants to make an underwater movie of the feat. But his offer of a large money reward goes unclaimed. Nobody will do it, not even to get rich.

However, islanders all over the Pacific are imaginative fishermen. After centuries of practice they have evolved some safe and novel methods. The way Kiribatians and the Tuvaluans catch flying fish and Samoans snare sharks are some examples.

Entire villages of people go to sea in boats just after sunset. They hoist the sails, which are V-shaped with the points downward. A man in each canoe holds a flaming torch. The fleet cruises over the water close together in a long line.

Flying fish, startled by the light, flip from the waves into the air. They are caught in the big, billowing sails. Soon the boats are full.

Flying fish.

Torch fishing for flying fish. Photograph by Gordon Gahan/P.R.

Samoans are fond of the meat of hammerhead sharks. This variety is odd-looking. Its head is shaped like a hammer with eyes on the ends of the strikers. Hammerheads are peaceable, but they grow big and put up a battle when caught.

Picture this scene in your mind: Two Samoan fishermen row out to sea in their little canoe. While one man paddles the other shakes a rattle in the water. This noisemaker is made of half coconut shells strung on a cord. They make a buzzing sound, like a school of fish.

With luck a triangular fin soon appears above the waves. But the shark is suspicious and swims in a wide circle around the boat.

The fishermen tie a heavy line onto a long pole. On the end of the line they attach a mullet fish. One of the men trails the bait in the water ahead of the canoe. The other holds a big loop of rope in readiness.

The shark finally goes for the mullet. The man with the pole moves it close to the boat. As the hammerhead swims by it is lassoed. The loop closes tightly around its neck in back of the protruding "hammer heads".

If the fishermen are expert they will quickly tie the shark to the boat. If not, the big fish will dive. When that happens, they have a fight on their hands. Sometimes it slips out of the noose and escapes.

That is how wise old fishermen deal with sharks. This is the story of how a 14 year-old boy in the Solomon Islands behaved with one.

He landed an eight foot gray shark with his bare hands!

His name was Joseph Bonie. One day he and several other boys his age were fishing close to shore. They put their baskets of fish in the shallow water to keep fresh. The shark was attracted by the smell of the fish and headed for them. It must have been very hungry. Sharks don't usually come that close to the beach.

Joseph caught it by the tail. He dragged it up the beach. It swung its head around and bit his ankle.

The boys killed it, and that night their families enjoyed tender shark steaks.

Hammerhead shark. Photograph by Russ Kinne/P.R.

Beach fishing is popular. Groups of people form large circles in the shallows. They walk toward each other beating the water with their hands. They close the ring and stand closely side by side. The trapped fish are scooped into baskets.

Semi-circular stone walls are built on beaches. When the tide goes out fish are trapped on the sand behind them.

A common sight is that of men spearing fish in beach water at night. They carry torches or lanterns to locate the sleeping fish.

Tuna fishing is exciting. Large groups of canoes full of men and boys go after them. The fish gather in large schools. The fishermen can tell where the schools are by the birds hovering over the water.

When in the middle of the school of fish, the fishermen cast shiny pearl shell lures with barbless hooks into the water. These are attached to short lines on long poles.

When the fish bite they are pulled through the air and into the boats. The hooks slide out of the fishes' mouth and are cast again and again. Soon the boats are full of the pretty, chunky skipjack or yellow-fin tuna.

Fishing is big with Pitcairn Islanders. There are only about 60 of these people, yet they catch more than 7,000 fish a year. Once three teenage boys caught 200 with hook and line in one day!

THE PEARL DIVERS OF MANIHIKI

Pearls! The very word reminds you of treasure. No matter how small, they are worth much money. They have always been considered beautiful and desirable. Women like to wear them in rings, pendants and necklaces. Kings include them among their crown jewels. No pirate's treasure chest would be complete without these softly glowing jewels of the sea.

Pearls are made by irritated oysters. A grain of sand gets inside the shell. This bothers the animal. It covers the itchy place with a hard, glossy substance. Usually the color is white or rosy. In rare cases it is black.

Round pearls are most valuable, but they grow in many shapes — oval, teardrop, flat and tube-like.

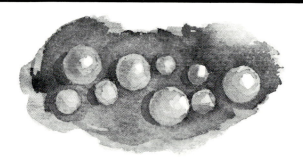

Half pearls . Photograph by Ann Morgan/P.R.

The pearlers paddled their canoes out to Manihiki Reef in the Cook Islands early in the morning. The sea was calm, the sun already hot. There were three or four to a boat, mostly men, but some women. One was the diver, the others paddlers and helpers. They had left the island beach at sunup. Before that they had attended church services.

When they got over the reef the divers slid into the water. They went straight down until they found the oysters clinging to the rocks. They pried the shells off and put them into baskets. When full, these were pulled up to the boats on ropes. Then the baskets were lowered, weighted with rocks to make them sink faster.

Some divers can hold their breath for as long as four minutes, so sometimes a diver would fill two baskets before rising to breathe. But mostly they would go up with each basketful.

The helpers opened the oysters and looked for pearls. Then they cleaned the shells of flesh and put them in sacks. Bright knives flashed in the sun. The workers sang and laughed. They shouted the news whenever a pearl was discovered.

All the shells are kept because they are the source of mother-of-pearl. They are more valuable than the pearls. The gems are few and far between.

There are two kinds of mother-of-pearl shell. The one with yellow edging is called gold-lip and the one with black is called black-lip. The gold-lip fetches the highest price.

Once thousands of pearlers searched for oysters in the Pacific. Now only a few engage in the dangerous task.

The biggest oyster beds are in the Cook Islands and in the Torres Straits, between Australia and Papua. For a while dredge-like machines were used to harvest the shells. But they broke the oysters and otherwise ruined the beds. Now most of the harvest is gathered by hand again.

PALOLO IS RISING!

The Pacific Ocean is much more beneficial to man than dangerous. It provides food of many kinds for the islanders. Besides fish it yields several kinds of edible worms. One of these is most unusual.

This sea-worm is called palolo. It looks like a thin strip of spaghetti about 18 inches long. Palolo lives on the sea bottom, attached to coral reefs. Twice a year it sets free its back portion, which rises to the surface of the sea. Its head part stays on the sea bottom and grows another tail.

Worms might not appeal to you as a source of food, but Samoans and Fijians love to eat palolo. They think it is the most delicious food of all.

Girl with Palolo worms. Photograph by James Siers.

When the palolo is rising in the sea off the beaches of Samoa and Fiji, the scene looks something like this: It is a little after midnight in October. The moon is three-quarters full. The beaches are crowded with islanders.

Men, women, boys and girls line the water's edge. Many of them are in canoes. All carry large woven leaf baskets and coarse cloth nets on handles.

Here and there the people gather around beach fires. They chat and sing. This is an exciting and happy occasion. It will last only a few hours this morning. The only other time of year it will happen again will be a month from now.

Palolo is rising!

Soon the sea will be covered with those mouth-watering tidbits.

Slowly the moon goes down and the sun comes up. As the dawn approaches the boats are rowed out to sea. People wade into the water. The tide is going out so they can go far away from shore. Now and then there is a gurgle and a splash as someone steps into a deep hole!

Everyone anxiously scans the surface of the sea. Nothing yet.

Then just before sunrise a shout goes up. Palolo! Palolo! Now the water is thick with wriggling green and brown worms.

Everyone scoops with dipnets and hands. Basket after basket is filled and taken to the beach. The harvesters work furiously because they have no more than one hour. By sunrise the palolo will be gone, sunk back into the sea.

Palolo worms are tasty fried or boiled into soup. Samoans relish them raw. Many eat their fill while gathering them. The catch is packed into many small leaf pouches. These are given to relatives and friends who cannot get to the sea.

Palolo is a wonder to science. This simple seaworm keeps both sun and moon time. It rises to the surface only two nights of the year, in October and November.

The moon directs its choice of the day. The sun controls its choice of the month. For two years it rises after 12 months. Every third year it rises after the 13th. Every 28 years it waits another 29½ days.

Why?

Bringing in the catch of Palolo.

Probably a combination of the sun's rays and the moon's pull on the tides. At a certain position the sun shines deep into the sea. It strikes the worm. The creature starts to let go of its tail.

The last dark quarter of the moon occurs when the tide is low. The water pressure is less then. The worm, already touched by the sunlight, lets its tail go. Up it floats to the surface of the sea.

These tails are full of eggs.

The male and female worms mix together in the water. When the sunlight gets warm it dissolves their containers. The green male eggs fertilize the brown female eggs. They sink to the bottom to hatch another generation of worms.

That is, those that are not eaten by the Samoans and Fijians!

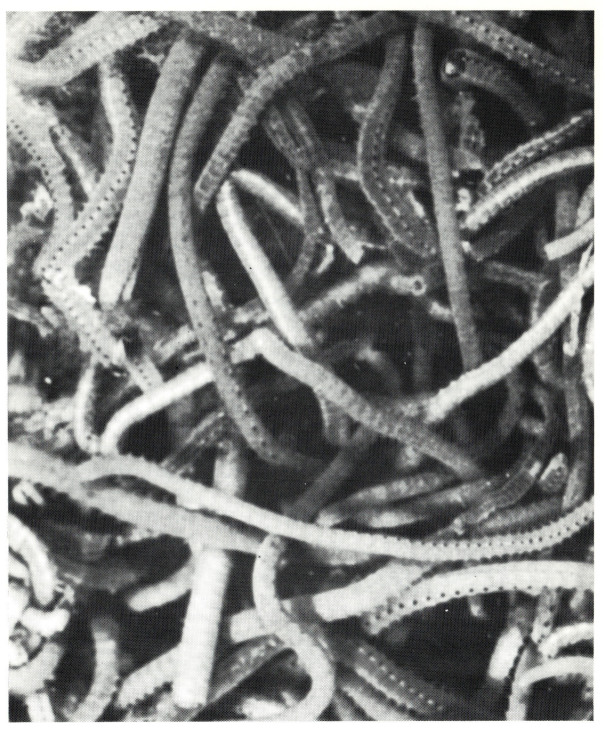

Palolo worms.